This illustration was done by Glenna L Gidley.

DEDICATION

First and foremost, I would like to thank the Living God for the privilege to create this work: for with Him nothing is impossible.

I would like to dedicate this effort to the three women in my life that have made it possible to possess the tenderness of spirit to feel, the development of the tools and the desire to put it into writing, and finally, the willingness and the desire to share it.

Carol Marie Gidley -Titko, my mother and first friend;

Natalie Durrant, my teacher and friend;

Patricia L Gidley, my wife and best friend.

I would also like to acknowledge the following for their contribution to this book.

Margo Bechio, who set a fine example.

Roy Ault, who freed me from writer's block.

Mary Crabtree, who helped me get off center.

Edythe & Gerald Burgess, for the gift of patience.

Of Love and Death
And
Lighter Things

AN ORIGINAL COLLECTION OF POEMS
AND OTHER WRITINGS

BY

RANDY DWIGHT GIDLEY

COPYRIGHT © 2012
BY
RANDY DWIGHT GIDLEY

ISBN 978-0-9647758-0-0
Library of Congress Control Number:
2013941577

PUBLISHED BY
THE GIDLEIGH PUBLISHING CO.
DELTONA FLORIDA

EXECUTIVE PRODUCER AND EDITOR
PATRICIA L. GIDLEY

COVER DRAWING
BY
JEFF FOURNIER
*

SELECT
ILLUSTRATIONS
BY
REBECCA WILCOX
*

GLENNA L. GIDLEY
*

JOHN P. GIDLEY
*

JULIE ANNE GIDLEY
&
And various other members of the Gidley Clan

Of Love

And Death

And Lighter Things

In addition, I have added a few snips of wisdom, an occasional thought and seasoned lightly with a dash of babble.

The night had turned nasty, as a
threatening storm finally broke. Now
and then, incandescent flashes of
lightning framed the old Victorian
manor perched high on the cliffs
above a churning sea.

Preface

I have only a vague memory of when I first started to write. I suspect it was when I first picked up a crayon and dutifully practiced my ABC's on the refrigerator door. As I would recall in later years, this particular experience would provide me with two of the many, if not invaluable lessons, that I would learn throughout my life. The first of these would be that writers tend to practice their craft whenever and wherever possible, and second, (at the time it seemed the more noteworthy) writing can be painful.

The beginning is irrelevant. I am more concerned with the present and future efforts, and ultimately the end. My "End" that is. (Don't you just hate it when someone ends a sentence with a verb?) Well, getting back to my narrative, to be sure I am a hopeless romanticist. As such, I can come up with some pretty colorful scenarios pertaining to my demise.

I can see the scene as it unfolds in my minds' eye:

It was a dark and stormy night. "Hold on, back off you hombres!!! Don't you be having any hissy-fit. (The previous deviation from proper grammar is sponsored by my poetic licenses.) Talk about plagiarism! OK! I just got caught up in the moment, I feel better now. I'll start over with something a little more original to set the proper mood.

The night had turned nasty, as a threatening storm finally broke. Now and then, incandescent flashes of lightning framed the old Victorian manor perched high on the cliffs, high above a churning sea.

A figure, its features cloaked against the chill, silently detaches itself from the shadows, and slips through an opening in the vine encrusted wall surrounding the estate. Quickly, it makes its way along the tree lined drive towards the main entrance. Climbing the steps, the intruder pauses as a bolt of lightning reveals a carving in the mantle of the doorway. "Windsweep," he reads. "Strange," he mutters to himself. Moving from shadow to shadow he slips around the corner and continues down the east side of the building until he is lost in the mist as the rain begins to fall harder. Amidst the clamor of

the storm, aided by the crashing waves below, the groan of a door opening goes unnoticed by those inside.

Within the ancient decaying walls, memories from the distant past, drifting by like dry thistles, borne by an unseen hand, float from room to room. Seemingly taking advantage of a crash of lightning, a greater darkness detaches itself from a doorway in the main corridor and makes its way towards a barely discernible glow that could be seen flickering from under the massive oak doors of the study at the far end of the passage. Reaching the portal, the visitor extends a gloved hand forward barely nudging the door. Ever so slightly… the great barrier swings in revealing the occupants.

Within the library, surrounded by toys and mementos collected from a lifetime of travel, I sit at my two-hundred year old roll-top desk. I am dressed in a worn, yet still elegant, tweed smoking jacket. I peck aimlessly at the keyboard of my trusty IBM clone. Nearby, my favorite "Homes brier" lazily smolders in an elephant-foot ashtray, its' sweet emissions adding balance to the musty dampness. In the corner, a grandfather clock goes about its' task of measuring my life, one second at a time. Softly, ever ticking … ticking…ticking, it pauses only long enough to announce the bewitching hour.

Aside from an occasional crackling sound coming from the fireplace, the only noise in the spacious apartments comes from Eva Ashley, my ever faithful housekeeper. Fussing about, she softly sings to herself. Now and then, my ears catch an escaping syllable, betraying a rich Blackpool accent. I am content. Having just brought my customary late-night hot cocoa, Eva's voice trails off to a whisper, as she is momentarily distracted by a meaningful clutter that I have left on the divan.

Looking up, in response to the hackles raising on the nape of my neck, I start to turn towards the doors from the corridor behind me. Before realizing the full implications of the widening gap in the study doors, the pressure hits. A searing torrent of anguish rips the breath from my lips as the betraying sound of death dies in my throat. As the darkness begins to sweep over me I reach for my ever present quill and parchment, treasured gifts from my children. I manage to scroll a few words before giving in to the pain, I lay my head down on my aching left arm. The last thing I am aware of, is clutching the organ that has betrayed me.

Miss Eva, unaware of the scene unfolding behind her, turns to protest my slovenly ways. Encountering my still form slumped over the keyboard of my computer, a transitory look, bordering on sadness, creeps across her face. Knowing this was inevitable, she slowly approaches the body of her beloved employer. Affectionately, she removes the ancient quill pen from the gnarled fingers of my dangling right hand. Under my left arm she notices a tattered piece of dried yellowed parchment. There, written in ornate script, three words stare up at her: "Roses in December." A puzzled expression distorts her face for a brief moment, then fades. As a single tear winds its' way down the curve of her cheek, she reaches for the telephone to notify the authorities of my untimely departure.

Deep within the gloom of the outer chamber, the midnight visitor is consumed by a terrible rage. Cheated of his revenge, he turns and stealthily creeps from the great hall.

Wow! Sounds impressive? (Pardon my bias.) Dare I say it sounds a little like Edgar P?" I should flatter myself so much! Bits and pieces of facts and fantasies, woven together like a spiders' web. Almost impossible to tell what belongs and what doesn't. If it were only true.

Actually, I don't, and never have smoked, hence the lack of need for pipes and elephant-foot ashtrays. Oddly enough, I do own a genuine boars-foot ashtray, (actually I have four of them, this being the number of feet the critter had at the time) a trophy of an early hunting episode. The narrative of which I shall endeavor to relate in such intimate detail in the not too distant future, as to demonstrate the foolishness of an impetuous youth. As for the mementos in question, three of these ended up in the Christmas stockings of my children, and the fourth, I keep jelly-beans in that one on my desk.

Getting back to my not smoking, that being the case, it's obvious that I wouldn't have need of a smoking jacket, elegant or otherwise. The closest thing I have is a ragged old terry-cloth bathrobe equally shared by myself, the boss, and our four children.

Now, as to a housekeeper, get serious! The only way I could afford one, would be if one would volunteer, and only then if he or she would provide their own transportation and meals. (Not being a sexist, I will gladly accept charity from anyone, regardless of gender. However, I do find it is a bit more pleasurable to show ones' profound gratitude to members of the opposite sex. All things being equal, I would rather offer a hug than a hand shake.) If, in the course set before me, I should encounter success, in the form of a "Best Seller" or some other form of literary note, and or state lotto, my position on the matter of home domestics might change.

Speaking of domestics, it would be sheer fantasy to expect a servant to fetch hot cocoa in the middle of the night to a crotchety old man, whether or not he was adored.

Last, but certainly not least, is the question of a computer. Look! It took me nearly ten years of nursing a self-imposed quasi wishy-washy attitude towards spending "family money" on myself, especially for something that promoted what could only be described as a hobby. (Ever notice that we tend to classify things we like to do in terms of "if it makes money its a profession, if it doesn't, it's a hobby.") In other words "diapers and milk" before "pen and ink" or PC. When I finally acquired a typewriter it was an old portable with an "e" key that stuck. (I never imagined the number of words in the English language containing the letter "e".) My top typing speed, using two fingers, was 20 words per minute. A couple years later, at a flea market, I got a sweet deal on a government retired IBM. That baby had everything! It was even equipped with a set of "GI" issued ear plugs; I think it needed a muffler or something. Top speed on that puppy was a blazing 40 words per. (Two fingers, plus thumbs.) As I approached my fifth decade, with three of my four children flushed from the nest, no easy task I might add, I finally bought my first PC, USED!!!

Regardless of where and when I began to write, or for that matter where it will end, it is of little or no importance.

The relevance lies in the fact that I do. The greater question is "why?"

I could bore you with tons of drivel about a fundamental urge compelling me to create something that would survive my passing. Something besides the cold facts routinely reported in the obits. William Shakespeare, dead these three hundred years, lives on in his written word. While I would never presume to compare what I write to that of the great "Bard," (I'm not that foolish.) like him, I have something to say, and like him, I choose to write it down. (So much for comparisons.) If just one person benefits, or is moved by what I write, then I feel that my effort was worth the time and energy I have expended. My one hope is that my descendants, upon reading my ramblings, find some value to them, and consider it my legacy. For God knows that I don't have much else to leave in the form of worldly goods. In "King John" Shakespeare wrote, "Life is as tedious as a twice told tale."

What can I say? There may not be any new plots left to discover, but at least I can have some fun adding some new wrinkles to the old standards. A night of watching television should convince the harden skeptic that it can be done. While it's easy to see how this has been accomplished in the field of drama, what about poetry? Roses are red etc., etc. In the case of rhyme, it becomes arduous trying to describe something that every poet has labored over ever since that Cro-Magnon painted a bison on a cave wall in France. After all, there are only so many ways to cook a potato.

To be sure you will find an occasional clover field, restless sea, or (shudder) Majestic Mountain, seasoning my writings, an inevitable fact of life. However, I try to limit myself to reporting only those things that have had a personal impact on me in my daily journey through this life. Most of these things that I chose to share come from within. Memories and thoughts some that date back to my earliest teens reflect an inner turmoil that at times frighten me. I like to think of myself as a poet. There have been some that have disputed that claim. Simply put, I love poetry. I must confess that most of what I read today, I don't understand. What I do, I like. A direct result, I believe, from a seed planted, low those many years ago, in a far off realm called "Central High," by a certain English teacher and mentor.

I know that I must live in the real world. How I view that world is up to me. I believe reality lies in the mind of the dreamer, lacking only an interpretation, a gentle dissection of the offering, allowing us to separate fantasy from reality, possible from the impossible, and truth from the lies. Only then, can we store it properly in the repository of the mind. There are side effects, pleasant ones for the gentler folk. Besides teaching us to use our imagination, it affords us a certain amount of relaxation, and entertainment. I write because it pleases me. The motives are my own. While some may find them interesting, they are harmless. There is a longing in me, an all-consuming hunger.

A cool autumn chill descends upon the land, promising an end to the dog days of summer. Deep within the forest, a fox squirrel pauses a moment from his labor of storing provisions for the coming winter, and lifts his nose to the wind. On a nearby lake, a great northern goose awakens from a late summer nap, his feathers tremble in anticipation of a long journey to a place he has never seen. A sense of urgency pervades his consciousness. It is a longing...a yearning, a task that must be performed.

I too, must perform. So I write, driven to a realm where the only limits are my imagination.

I believe reality lies in the mind of the dreamer, lacking only an interpretation.

Of Love

Love, let me count the ways, so says the poet. Sweet, sugar coated words that invade the heart. They quicken the pulse, and add blush to the cheek. Two lovers stroll down a pristine beach, hand in hand, at sunset. Their love inspiring such passionate emotions, that their imagination lifts them higher and higher into the nether realms.

Love comes in all shapes and sizes, colors and textures. It is a tapestry woven of emotions that envelops its very creator often giving purpose for its existence.

But in order to love, there must be an object of that love. In my case, there is Trish. Trish...my sweet Trish. If I but possessed the whole world, I would gladly lay it at her feet. We are forever soul-mates. Our spirits are so entwined; we are as one, each the sum-total of the whole. It should not come as a surprise that most of what I write is for, or about her.

Love has been compared to a rose. As beautiful as it is, one must be aware of the thorns. Cultivated properly, it can grow into a thing of beauty, and be a constant source of pleasure for a lifetime. Spurn it, and it will grow into a wild tempestuous thing that can prick the soul and leave scars on the heart.

THE MAIDEN THAT CHALLENGED
THE SEA

She stood there in silent anger.
Before her the mighty ocean whispered:
"I am the restless sea, come, let me touch your soul.
I will give of myself
Such bounty that will feed your multitudes,
And quiet their pains of desire."

She answers:
"Roll on, restless sea, touch not the soul of my love.
Such cruelty concealed within your murky depths
That reaches forth with icy fingers to seize
Those brave mortals that venture forth
To reap their just harvest."

Again there came a whisper:
"I am the restless waves.
Come, let me touch your soul,
See what bounty I display ?
Come choose what you will.
My coffers are everlasting."

Her reply was swift:
"Roll on, restless waves, touch not
The soul of my love.
I have seen the broken gifts you offer,
Disfigured things that once possessed life's spark,
Twisted forms swept back and forth in mock imitation,"

 Presently, the wind picked up and paused at her ear.
"I am the restless wind, come, let me touch your soul.
I bring fragrance from the South China Sea.
My trade winds will fill your sails,
Carrying you forth to seek out the mystery of Cathay."
She shook her head and acknowledged:

"Roll on, restless wind,
"Touch not the soul of my love,
I have heard the moans and sobs of despair.
I have inhaled your sweet temptations,
And felt your gentleness stroke my hair."

Together they came to her.
"I am the restless sea, come give up the land.
I am the restless waves, come, let me carry you away.
I am the restless wind, come, feel my cleansing breath"
A mute rage swelled within her breast.
Clenching her fist, she roared:

"Roll on, restless sea, I will not give up my love,
I will smooth his brow with such tenderness,
That will turn his thoughts
From your coral encrusted treasures.
I will use such persuasion that would fire
The very cauldrons of hell."

"Roll on, restless waves,
I will not give up my love.
I will turn his eyes from your beckoning call,
I will hold him fast within passions grip,
I will warm his bed with my flesh,
That he would remember your cool breath."

"Blow on, restless wind, I will not give up my love .
I will chain him with the seeds of his likeness,
I will whisper desires that promise more than your siren's wails"
At last, her anger spent, she mocked:
Each day of our lives, together,
We will stand in the sight of your majesty and give thanks.
But I will not give up my love."

WHAT IS THY NAME?

What is thy name?
You, who ease the pains of day to day,
And smooth the hurt of failures.
You, who draw the burning,
From my soul's self-doubts.
Thy name is Comfort.

What is thy name?
You, who bring laughter to my tired mind,
And smiles to my lips.
You, whose twinkling eyes and mischievous grin
Betray some surprise you have in store for me.
Thy name is Joy.

What is thy name?
You, who take the blunt of my cruel criticisms,
And suffer the humiliation born
Of my raving and frustrations.
Thy name is Loyalty

.What is thy name?
You, whose desires overwhelm my manhood,
With the fire in your bosom and love in your heart;
Whose clinging chains of passion
Keep me ever your obedient servant.
Thy name is Love.

And thus I ask, what is thy name?
Thy name is *Wife!*

LONELY CHILD

When I was young
And the world was new,
You found me and I found you.
I was a hope-filled child, I know,
For finding you had made me so.

Hand in hand we walked the fields,
Exchanging kisses for daffodils.
I was a carefree child, I know,
For holding you had made me so.

Then came the day you took my hand,
The promise made of a golden band.
I was a joy-filled child, I know,
For having you had made me so.

Then I gave all, my everything.
You gave nothing… only pain.
I was a heart-sick child, I know,
For trusting you had made me so.

I walk the fields,
My head held high.
I walk alone. I will not cry.
I am a lonely child, I know,
For loving you, has made me so.

DON'T PICK THE FLOWERS

How like the flowers upon the hill
So proud and free you stand,
Loved by some, admired by all,
Yet, you ask no grace from man.

How strange these feelings that you stir
Within my poets' mind,
To walk with you in clover fields
And brush your hand with mine.

Could I but touch you more gently
Than the thistle tossed by the wind.
Could I but love you more truly
And still remain just a friend.

For oh sweet child, I must not touch
That which my heart doth hold.
I must not desire what cannot be
And create a tortured soul.

For, tis wrong indeed to lock away
That which longs to dance,
To hold but for a single day
A flower that blooms but once.

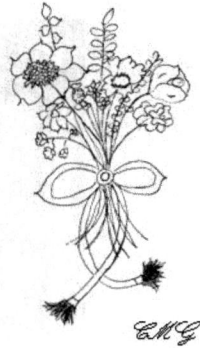

EMG

FAITHFUL I

How still I sit on darken hill
 Watching the stars drift by.
   I hear the song of the cricket
     And the chirp of his mournful cry.

     Take hold, quivering breast,
       That I might say
     The things that must be said.
    For in my heart the words do lay,
 Hidden emotions that I dread.

  For love has withered
   Where once it bloomed,
      Through still in faith am I.
      I'll lock away these things unsaid,
        Til the stars fall from the sky.

A TRILOGY OF TEARS

EARTH MOTHER

Our Earth Mother is weeping
Her tears are blessed,
From this gentle falling rain
Springs the harvest from her breast.

STOUT HEART

Though stout and bold my heart my be
It knows no earthly fear,
Yet the gentle caress of a maiden's kiss
It melts before her tears.

TOUCH OF FORGIVENESS

I have longed the cool touch of forgiveness
As sin came between over the years,
In humility I seek the Face of God,
In sorrow I would morn His tears.

Lucy

What can we say
Who love you so,
Those you leave behind.
Each of us embroidered so
On the tapestry of your mind.

For countless years you've healed our hurts
And wiped away our tears,
Your soothing words have calmed our hearts
And laid aside our fears.

What can your worth or measure be
What payment could we deed,
To one who shares unselfishly
To those of us in need.

But dear sweet Lucy, can't you see
With all your healing arts,
There is one pain you can not heal
That, the breaking of our hearts.

But rest assured you safely dwell
Within our fondest dreams,
With moisten eyes and heavy hearts
We yield to heavens schemes.
For in the end, when all is said
Though sad we all may be,
Wiser and healthier that we are
For having been touched by thee.

AND DEATH

It truly seems odd that it requires such a traumatic event, such as death, to stimulate creativity in the poets' pen. All the greats, from William Cullen Bryant to Edgar Allan Poe, have been touched by death in one way or another and have come away profoundly changed by it.

Such bittersweet thoughts that momentarily hold us in tow, it reddens and swells the eye with tears and grief, while clutching at the heart with talons of guilt. Death is all around us. It is a constant part of the living universe. We are confronted by it daily. It lies at the very edge of our senses, a constant reminder of our own mortality. From the rust on our cars, to the cow patiently awaiting the final journey through the "Golden Arches", we are all faced with the prospect of an end to something or someone we love and cherish.

So, let us take heart, and press on into the valleys of purple shade, pause a moment, take a deep breath, then quickly move on.

WHO CARES?

When your tears go unnoticed
And your smiles go unseen,
When your questions go unanswered
And your heart gives up its dream.
When days are long and dreary
And the nights laced with fear,
And those you love forget you
And the longing for friends disappear.
When laughter is met with silence
And your words fall on deaf ears,
When all seems lost and you ponder
On the mistakes you've made o'er the years.

Just remember there's always someone
That will help you remake,
That precious gift of hope you've lost
And forgive that one mistake.
For believing your tears go unnoticed
And your smiles go unseen,
And for thinking they've all forgotten
And for giving away your dreams.
So bow your head in reverence,
Lift up your hands in prayer.
And shame on you for doubting
In the end, it's God who cares.

JPG

INFINITES' GATE

Oh, what glory that man knows
When at first he struggles to hold,
That by which his strength has won.

Could he but see the havoc wrought
Must he be told what price he's lost
Of what the need and what the cost?

Blind to all that is not good
He turns from truth instead,
To choose, then dwell upon his bed

Tis sad indeed, when youth has fled
And lesser things are chosen instead
To fill those wells of trust with dread
Now hope is gone and love is dead.

Speak softly, nothing is wrong,
Only spring and summer are gone,
Fall and winter will not be long.
Dream on and on and on...

WHO WILL REMEMBER ?

Who will remember
Now that you are gone?
You that lie beneath the changeless ground,
Yet we are the ones that wronged.

Who will remember your shy smile
Your wisdom and your grace?
Who will remember the tender kisses
Gently placed upon my face ?

For all that has been is gone now
And all that will be is yet,
But, who will remember?
"I will, Mother, I won't forget."

SHADOW SELF

I am sickened even unto my soul,
As my shadow self morns
The unborn children of my fantasies,
Lamenting unplanned campaigns
And wars that will never be fought.
The gauntlet of daily challenges
Lies ignored at my feet.
Dreams that have rotted away for lack of use
Clutter my vision of reality,
With the painful memories
Of my sweet youth when I knew hope.
Somewhere deep within
Those gothic cathedrals of my imagination,
Where only the unbridled mind may venture.
There lies submerged in thought
A truth I dare not utter.

For it is not that,
Of which I have never done
That saddens me.
But the thought of that
Of which I may never do.

SOMETHING IS MISSING

At first there were no tears,
Nor grief, nor pain,
Only a terrible feeling of loss.
It's like when you mislay a cherished memory
And can't remember.
A piece of the whole was gone.
Part of me is lost.

I seem to have misplaced something.
Where are my keys?
That's it!...I've lost my keys.
But...no, they are here,
Safely tucked within the hollow of my hand.
I have held them so tight, they have cut my palm.
Strange, there is no pain, nor hurt,
There is only...numbness.

The light comes and goes,
And comes again.
As I am gently rocked to and fro
In my land-locked ship,
There are no thoughts, nor feelings.
There is only a blackness.

Time is a dutiful servant,
Needing no direction
As it goes about its' job,
Of measuring my life.
One of many, even a season can become lost.
Has it been a year?
It seems only yesterday I lost...what?

What was the thing I was searching for?
I am drawn downstairs to the basement.
I descend the stairs into the gloom.

As I stand before a long neglected cupboard,
I force myself to breathe.
Slowly, I open the door and peek within.
On a shelf lies a faded blue stocking cap.
A sudden and terrible pain fills my being,

As the searing truth of reality engulfs my soul.
Torrents of tears cascade down
Through my fingers onto the floor.
My sanity, fighting for existence… holds
A mournful utterance of grief exhales
Betraying the thing I had lost.

Oh my God! My God! It's Papa!

I AM TUCKEE MANA

Where are the hills so green I climbed
And the amber fields I roamed,
Where flow the streams that quenched my thirst
And the forest I called my home?

Where are my furred brothers,
The beaver and buffalo I stocked?
Where dwells the mighty eagle,
And the salmon that he caught?

Where have the rushing waters gone,
That fed the honeycomb pine?
Where is this land they promised us,
For as long as the sun would shine?

My spirit is saddened by what I see
For dead are the things I love,
Long gone the scream of the red tailed-hawk,
And the coo of the morning dove.

Gone are the Gods that loved this land,
That blessed it with their own.
Gone the children they loved the most,
And the freedoms that they've known.

I am he who is called Tuckee Mana.
This song I leave behind.
When I am gone no tears will flow,
To mourn this land of mine.

For gone is the wandering red-man
And those who were his kin.
Only the memories are left behind,
To remind us of the sin.

Memories are those precious things
That reminds us of the past.
We shelter those we love the most,
And keep the best for last.

Come join with me, my brothers
Let us speak of our place of birth,
For the night is long as we sing our song,
Of the death of Mother Earth.

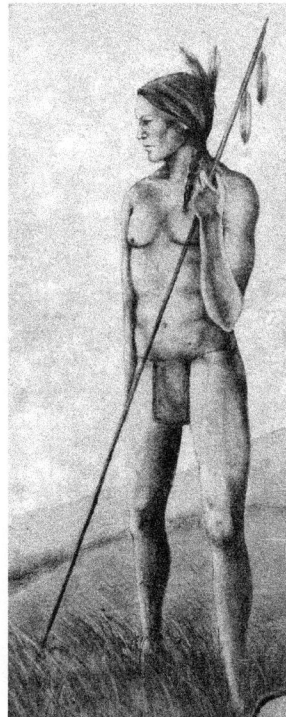

AFTER THOUGHT

The dust lies heavy upon my brow
While in this grave I lie
A thousand years this night has seemed
For peace has passed me by.

A million voices cry out in pain,
A million souls have sinned
A million thoughts bridge time and space
Where will the torment end ?

The chill does seep into my form
While the silence claws the brain,
For gone the sunny warmth of life,
Nothing remains the same.

Grieve not for me, for I am dead,
But for those that must live on,
For it is they that mournfully tread
To the wail of the banshees' song.

ODE TO MERCUTIO

Though the years be great,
And time has passed,
The tears still swell within.
For the heart remembers
What the mind forgets,
Of the pain that covers the sin.

For great the family Montague,
Many the joys they knew.
For deep within the oyster lies,
A pearl of magnificent hue.
Youth the treasure, we strive to protect
Thus guard against the blade,
For rashly put, an unkind word,
Doth sever the greatness made.

For as the night, envies the day
To meet, as the sun doth set.
So had the clan of Montague,
In the house of Capulet.
Within this tempest the torrents rage
Such things that man must do
With blade in hand, did Tybalt take,
The life of a Montague

Oh Mercutio, dear Mercutio,
How rashly you did live.
Tis true, tis true, yet pale you lay,
Slain for a Montague.
But for the courage love hath made,
Poor Romeo's fate should be,
The same as he whose blood did flow,
For an end he could not see.

Revenge is sweet I've heard it said,
Though the price may fan the strife.
So did the lovesick Romeo's sword,
Did take young Tybalt's life.
For within this tale there lies a truth,
That must be taught and learned.
For rashly put the spoken word,
Doth scar the heart concerned.

This poem was first written by my daughter Julie, when she was a freshman in high school. I assisted her in converting it to Shakespearian English with modifications.

Lighter Things

While love and death may provoke a strong emotion from each of us, it is levity that revitalizes the soul. Love helps us to see the beauty in the world, while mirth helps us to appreciate it.

Death...accents reality, laughter helps us to deal with the inevitable.

Time, the great equalizer, may heal all wounds, but just try to keep a straight face when the "Black Knight" (From Monty Pythons' "The Holy Grail") informs King Arthur that his freshly severed limbs are but "a mere scratch," and then discloses, "I've had worse". This might suggest that, even in the midst of a tragedy , by poking fun, it might somehow anesthetize us and speed up the healing process. So permit me to offer a dose of light prose, some thought-provoking , some idealistic, some just plain fun. Enjoy!

WHAT PRICE?

What price would you pay
For a morning so clear,
That a single breath of cool crisp air
Brings joy to your lungs ?

What price would you pay
To dip your finger in a crystal stream
And feel the cool liquid fall in drops
To your thirsty tongue ?

What price would you pay
To once again walk
The fields and forest of your youth
With strong and steady strides?

Is there a price too high or a cost so great?
I have walked the trail on a warm day
With brother scouts,
Staff in hand
And a song in my throat.

I have reached out in compassion
And tied the knot of friendship
With those I have shared
Love of land, water and sky.

When life's' day is done
And I sit around the campfire with my fellows.
We will talk of trails, streams, and hills.
We will remember our youth,
When summers were long and hot
And the days seemed endless,
And we were immortal.

What price would I pay, you ask?

Why, all that I have.

Written for Billy Y, (The Eternal Boy Scout)

I WONDER

Who can help but wonder
What life is all about,
When days are filled with surprises
Harboring hopes and doubts.

If I but knew the purpose
If I could guess the end,
I wouldn't leave this life in doubt
Of what had never been.

Oh, lucky are they that know their worth,
But luckier still am I,
For I have asked, and been told the truth
And know the reason why.

For each of us is special
And the difference is plain to see,
Each of us can proudly say,
God only made one of me.

FROM WHERE THE WIND BLOWS FREE

Cool the night breeze blowing
Gentle fragrance from the sea,
Scent, from the realm of "Moby Dick"
From where the wind blows free.

From where the wind doth kiss the shore
And waves and winds are born,
Once sailed the mighty long boats
To the blare of the Viking's horn.

For many are the tales about the sea
And many the good ships in her deep,
For brave were the men that challenged her waves
And cold is the watch they keep.

DOWN FROM THE NORTH

Down from the north, they came in force
Vengeance in their eyes,
None could stay, their might that day
And all who opposed would die.

The earth trembled as they passed
Their deeds scarred the land,
For none cold stop the bloody horde
Of the man called Genghis Kahn.

Crimson flowed upon the ground
Streams of blood ran red,
Suffering and anguish was everywhere
Til all who opposed were dead.

My very soul did quake with fear
As my body did tremble and sway,
I could not look, so I closed my book,
And quickly put it away.

ODE TO A GHOSTY

Oh, what shimmering light comes dancing?
Twix tombstones this moon-filled night,
What mischievous trickery planned?
To pale me thus in frozen flight.

Perchance some ghostly rattle of chains
Or moans of ghoulish delight,
Thus weakening the heart and raising the nape
To temp the vampires bite

Or could perhaps a hidden smile
Unseen by those about,
An impish grin or Younkers' sne
Testament to a living sprout.

For methinks there lurks within
A spirit that giggles so,
His aim to send me racing home
His secrets ne'er to know.

THE SEARCHING SOUL

Through the valley filled with night
Passed hills drenched in purple shade,
Over the mountains void of light
I searched for where my dreams are made.

On and on I searched in vain
For ne'er a clue I found,
Till at last I paused to rest
And heard a magic sound.

"Wake up, dear! You'll be late for school."

REMEMBER WHEN

I had a thought just the other day
Of things long ago,
The feeling passed, it did not last,
But left behind a glow.

It reminded me of simpler times
When as a youth I would,
Go searching secrets in the wilds
Of hills, lakes and woods.

And I remember when contentment was...

The warmth of the sun, when day was done
The sound of rain on tin,
Goldenrods and clover fields,
Stars and boyhoods friends.

Crystal dawns, and manicured lawns,
Dew dripping from a fern,
Ghostly lights on moon-filled nights
And fragrant leaves as they burn.

Skipping stones, and robins homes,
Pussy willows in the wind at play,
A rickety old barn, a cat name Tom,
And the smell of fresh-cut hay.
Of ice-clad hills, and winter chills
The hiss of a coon at bay,
Snowball fights, and winds that bite
And geese that honk all day.

It's nice to know that even though
It's been a while since then,
As time slips by with ne'er a sigh,
I can still remember when.

MORSELS

Oh, what long-forgotten wonders
Filtering down through moist laden air
Pausing but a brief moment at my nose,
Before moving on.

What spicy remembrances from my frenzied youth
Does it bear,
Transporting me back to those crystal clear morns,
When all seemed right and nothing amiss.

Such sights and sounds my mind conjures up
To remind me of a better place and time.
As I vainly grasp at fleeting shades,
That scurry away to seek refuge within
The secret recesses of my soul.

A constant reminder of buried treasure.
Those delicate morsels of wealth
That patiently wait to spring forth
At the first beckoning call
Of a long-forgotten sight, sound, or smell.

Pop Titko

I remember as a child my father telling us many stories to illustrate lessons we would learn in life. Many the times, I would just sit there shaking my head, wondering where in the world he came up with such wisdom, for you see, Pop didn't finish school. He left Central High School, in Columbus Ohio, in his sophomore year, to join the Civilian Conservation Corp, to help support his family. Over the years, I have gleaned much from his homespun wisdom. Moreover, I would like to think, made some slight improvements, only in the sense that times have changed, and I have merely put a new spin on these eternal truths.

One in particular concerned what kind of person I wanted to be known as. He told me there were mainly two types of people in the world, those that upon entering a room, people would turn smile and say "Looks who's here!" And then there are those that upon entering a room, people turn away and exclaim "Oh no, look who's here!" This truism had a great influence in my life, as I strived to be the first example. However, over the years I have observed a curious thing. Apparently there is a third group, and because of their very nature, are virtually unknown. These are those people that upon entering a room nobody notices or comments. How sad! To slip through life, unseen, unnoticed, unappreciated, and yes, sometimes unloved.

Lives of great men all remind us
We can make our lives sublime,
And, departing, leave behind us
Footprints on the sands of time"
— Henry Wadsworth Longfellow (Poems of Henry Wadsworth
Longfellow)

And ....

Tell me not, in mournful numbers,
Life is but an empty dream!
For the soul is dead that slumbers,
and things are not what they seem.
Life is real! Life is earnest!
And the grave is not its goal;
Dust thou art; to dust returnest,
Was not spoken of the soul.
— Henry Wadsworth Longfellow (Poems of Henry Wadsworth
Longfellow

Now for another surprise! Over the years Pop quoted from both
of these poems. Not the whole poem, and not verbatim, but just
enough to recognize the author. I am who I am because of two
men, James Dewitt Gidley, who gave me life, and Louis Titko
who taught me what to do with it. I am doubly blessed.

Randy Dwight (Titko) Gidley

Epilogue

As I draw this effort to a close, I cannot help but feel a bit sad. Not because it hasn't been fun or exhilarating, and there were times when it was particularly satisfying, yet, as with all things, it has had its' ups and downs. My sadness (here the word panic may be substituted) lies in the fact that I must now go on, having completed the first of two great Herculean tasks that I had set for myself in my youth. I must now complete the second, henceforth known as "THE NOVEL".

It has taken me over thirty-five years to arrive at the completion of the first labor, that of putting together a collection of my poetry. Judging from my past performance, I am not particularly encouraged. Applying the same time scale to "THE NOVEL" and factoring in momentum, I should   finish "Windsweep" (working title) sometime well into the next century, say just in time to celebrate the opening of Disney World's newest theme park... on the moon.

I assure you, I have always performed with the noblest of intentions in mind. God only knows, I have had tons of support over the years. I wouldn't go so far as to suggest that I procrastinate. Nothing could be further from the truth; actually, I am quite industrious. It's just that I'm easily distracted.

To illustrate the point, once while mowing the grass, I noticed that one of the wheels on my mower was rolling a bit rough. Leaving the mower running, I went to the garage to get some oil. While rummaging about in a cabinet, I found a spool of wire. A thought suddenly occurred to me, I had seen one of the rose bushes out in the front yard drooping. I envisioned a sort-of trellis made out of wire that would support the roses and allow them to climb. It would be easy to make, and connecting it to the over-hang of the roof would only take moments. But first, I needed to cut the wire into the various lengths. Remembering that I had seen the wire cutters in the kitchen drawer, I went to the house to retrieve them. Trish, seeing me banging about the drawer, asked me what I was doing. I explained that I was looking for the wire cutters. She informed me she had picked them up off the floor in the laundry room, where I had been working on the timer of the washing machine. Grabbing a cup of coffee on the way,

I went to the laundry room to retrieve the cutters. I found the cutters where Trish had laid them on the top of the washer. Picking them up, I noticed that they were quite warm. Feeling the top of the washer with my hand, I was not surprised to find it hot. "The timer!" I muttered, "It must have shorted out again. I had better take it off and have a look." I went back to the garage to get a screwdriver. In less than an hour, I had the problem fixed. Finishing, I put away my tools, washed up, and sat down to dinner. Later that evening, at my wife's prompting; I took the trash out to the curb for the morning pick-up. In the dark, I tripped over the lawn mower sitting where I had left it earlier in the day. Expelling articulations of a negative connotation and feeling a bit foolish, I grabbed it and began shoving it towards the garage. As I pushed it up the driveway, I noticed that one of the wheels was sticking.

Much of my life has followed this route, not that I haven't contributed to the confusion. I have been blessed with a vivid imagination, and some say, the lack of discipline to control it. As a youngster in school, I was the one that spiced up the teachers' prosaic dialog with gems of trivia, gleaned from dog-eared comic books (most notable were the "Harvard Classics," with an occasional foray into the "Lost Land with Turok Son of Stone") and then there was that never ending source of trivia, the "boob tube." (Here I wish to take the opportunity to declare my membership in the fraternal order of "Trekies & Trekers." Actually I pre-date Star Trek by a decade. I was bumming around the galaxy with the likes of Flash Gordon, Captain Video, and Rocky Jones, Space Ranger. Gosh! That was before hyper drive and warp field technology. While I considered this impromptu diversion during class generous on my part, and I'm not discounting the occasional nod of approval from the teacher, it unfortunately earned me the scorn of my classmates. In a misguided act of juvenile retribution, I was tagged "Mr. Know-it-all." A name, I might add, I wore proudly. I got even by becoming the teachers' pet. An occupation that most of my peers shunned like fried zucchini, I found quite profitable, especially around grading time. (My mama didn't raise up no dummy.)

In defense, I can only say I have grown emotionally, if not wiser in the ways of the world, or at least my small corner of it. I have learned one irrefutable fact, and that is that everything and everyone changes and that includes me. Sometimes it's for the better, sometimes not. Circles within circles, ever rotating, matching, mismatching, aligning and realigning, order out of Chaos. Fate? Hardly! Luck or providence, take your pick! I believe life is a stream of endless final exams, a contentious solving of daily problems. Problems that run the gauntlet of the common everyday boring variety, to the wildly imaginative forays into the surreal, they all contain certain elements that are unique to each of us. That's really what it's all about, problem solving, a never ending string of multiple choices.

In that vein, I now choose to end this aimless prattle. I really must get on with "THE NOVEL." But first, I think I'll take a little breather and help my granddaughter with her homework. She mentioned something about needing to write a poem.....

**To boldly go where the only limits,
are your imagination.**

Gidleigh Publishing

www.ingramcontent.com/pod-product-compliance
Lightning Source LLC
Chambersburg PA
CBHW071023040426
42443CB00007B/914